GOD

The Marriage & The Competition

By

Melvin Prince Johnakin

God, The Marriage & The Competition

Copyright 2023 by Melvin Prince Johnakin

All rights reserved. No part of this publication may be reproduced, distributed, or transmitted in any form or by any means, including photocopying, recording, or other electronic or mechanical methods, without the prior written permission of the publisher, except in the case of brief quotations embodied in critical reviews and certain other noncommercial uses permitted by copyright law.

Although the author and publisher have made every effort to ensure that the information in this book was correct at press time, the author and publisher do not assume and hereby disclaim any liability to any party for any loss, damage, or disruption caused by errors or omissions, whether such errors or omissions result from negligence, accident, or any other cause.

Adherence to all applicable laws and regulations, including international, federal, state and local governing professional licensing, business practices, advertising, and all other aspects of doing business in the US, Canada or any other jurisdiction is the sole responsibility of the reader and consumer.

Neither the author nor the publisher assumes any responsibility or liability whatsoever on behalf of the consumer or reader of this material. Any perceived slight of any individual or organization is purely unintentional.

The resources in this book are provided for informational purposes only and should not be used to replace the specialized training and professional judgment of a health care or mental health care professional.

Neither the author nor the publisher can be held responsible for the use of the information provided within this book. Please always consult a trained professional before making any decision regarding treatment of yourself or others.

Dedication

To all the men that are divorced from a marriage where they had to be in competition.

Forward

Men initiate the act of reproduction. Therefore, if a population is fearful of its genetic annihilating, it has to focus only on the men of the potentially annihilating population. When you consider an African man, African woman, European man, and European woman, there are four possible heterosexual combinations, but only one will produce a child with genetic makeup similar to European:

1) African man - African woman = dominant genes
2) African man - European woman = dominant genes
3) European man - African woman = dominant genes
4) European man - European woman = dominant genes

Neely Fuller Jr. - United Independent Compensatory Code/ System/System/Concept.

                    This statement is from Jawanza Kunjufu

Table of Contents

Forward 3
Introduction 5
Chapter One - When A Man Finds A Woman 8
Chapter Two - The Woman as a Leader 11
Chapter Three - The Misconception 14
Chapter Four - Follow The Leader 18
Chapter Five - Bible References to Marriage 20
Chapter Six - The Blind Leading the Blind 23
Chapter Seven - The Pillars of God and Marriage 26
Chapter Eight - When All Is Said and Done 29
About The Author 30

Introduction

How many times does it take before you realize that you're not the solution to a problem when it comes to marriage? You're not even the right person to give advice when asked. This is how the world treats someone who has never been married, yet these are the first people who are asked when there is a problem in a marriage.

Let's analyze this concept for a moment.

One, who told you to get married in the first place, was it God or was it your decision?

Two, why did you get married? Was it for love or money, or even some other reason?

Three, the one who says, "I DO" may just be saying that because they "Don't" want to be alone.

Find out where your inside told your outside that marriage was the right thing for you. The outcome may help you determine and help you realize who was the real person who kept you in a place where you did not belong and who wanted to have someone, they could just boss around.

You may find that when released from a marriage that was not yours to begin with or was not in its proper time will always result in turmoil and even misery in some cases. In others there could be a reunion as a friend or even a person who wants to be a husband without the paperwork. Either way somebody must change and there is never a clear picture of who that is when it comes to a marriage.

What if it's both of you and you don't even know it until you are alone and have had time to assess what really happened? The real truth about your marriage comes from God and he is a marriage counselor from the inside and of course he does solo sessions when you make your appointment.

In time, all marriages are more than meets the eye. They are happy, sad, moody, loving, and even impossible but never blame each other for what you think the other person should or should not be doing. You're not the boss of anything but yourself. You're not even the boss of that either without God so take a step back and get together with him to get the answers to the who, what, and whys of your life. Your marriage is not the whole picture, it's just a minor adjustment to the bigger plan which you were supposed to understand first, marriage second, and Love until death do you part third.

The single humans are not in the wrong for being single, they are in it to win it, with or without the other person to make them feel whole.

Two do become one but not without God as the merger and until you merge with God first, you're going in circles.

Chapter One

When A Man Finds A Woman

When a man finds a woman, he finds a good thing and he tells himself that over and over until he believes it in his heart. The next wonderful thing is the way he gets to express that to her/him night after night. The way a marriage starts is much like how we approach any new shiny event in our lives. We are excited, emotional, and ready to just do whatever it takes to be in the moment. Wow! What a feeling that is. The first lady and her man are just the way they are meant to be. Happy, healthy, and full of love. Courtesy is at its prime and the words flow freely on all topics. Talking all night, hoping for more. Just kissing and making love until the point of exhaustion. Just like he thought about night after night.

Her dream has come true, she has her knight in shining armor right by her side giving her everything she ever wanted. Wow! What a feeling that is! She is cooking whatever he wants, dressing all cute, never farting or doing anything that would make him go "Wait what." All the bills are being paid, and she can do whatever she wants when she wants to. No questions asked.

The next day comes and provides new opportunities to do the same, however little by little things get out of hand. She has new hobbies, new friends, and a newfound purpose in life. He has new expectations, and more money is needed to run the household and when the blessing of a child is introduced things really get a bit more challenging.

Now when does it become the job of the wife to also be the man of the house? Why does the day to day require two opinions vs one. And who is supposed to have the final say so. I was. Or so I thought. If you ask the other person, they will say God has the final word. So how do you argue with that. How do you compete with God and why do we have to?

The Bible does say the wife will submit to the husband but not the way I thought. The best thing that came out of this was to understand that if a wife is not married to her husband or the husband is not married to his wife and they are married to God, then can there be too much God in a marriage? How does one proceed in the marriage when all you say and do means nothing if it's not what is being understood by both. Where do you go for answers? A therapist, a counselor, or God.

Finding your place in a marriage can be difficult but if you come home every day and do what you were taught to do then there will be problems.

The husband and wife both have brought to the marriage most of what they learned from their parents or someone close to them. Society plays a big role in setting expectations for your relationship. I am not here to say I have the answers but everyone who is married is not telling the truth when they leave the house.

Chapter Two

The Woman as a Leader

The change of life is when a woman reaches her maturity level and then has to reset her internal panel, but when there is a change in who is the leader of the home it's another story. Not one that makes for a happy family and especially the man of the house.

One way to know if you're the man of the house is to make a decision and see if everyone stays the way of the decision. If not, then you are not only the man of the house you're the woman of the house too. The woman is supposed to be the fast follower of her husband at least that is what the Bible tell us. The other side of the coin is when the woman is the man, but she still wears a dress. The more confused men get the more they start to find a way out. If a man can't be a man in his own house, he will find a home where he can be and that may even be a different address. This is not always the case but there are many times when this is the outcome.

Since men have the need to be leaders, they are never at peace when the woman takes that role. It makes a man feel less than a man. If not a man, then what is left. The fight begins, the movement of time between the couple gets wider and the communications turns into arguments with no real winner.

A purpose for having a man in the house is to be the leader, protector, and knight in shining armor just like God made us. Having a woman try to take that role can be frustrating but also make you wonder why you are there.

A woman sees this as new territory but makes her way as best she can. There is no real desire to be the man of the house but when certain expectations, right or wrong are not met their instinct is to do it herself. This is part of the problem.

Expectations of what a man is supposed to do vs a woman can be quite a controversy but, in my world, chores are things that can be done by anyone. If you and your spouse are fighting about household chores, don't. Just agree to disagree and move on. Hire someone to help if needed.

The end game for a man is to be just what he was designed to be, the man of the house and if there is no man then there is no house at least not the way it started.

If God tells us in the Bible that a woman should submit to her husband and she decides that God is her husband, can there be too much God in a marriage?

God is in our marriages no matter what so what is the worst that can happen, you can get a divorce, but she stays married to God or you can ask God how to improve your role. Either way the answer lies with God.

Chapter Three

The Misconception

The biggest part of being married is understanding each other outside as well as inside. The ups and downs can be a challenge, however if you learn how to keep each other happy on the inside the outside will take care of itself.

When you take the vow to stay with someone for richer or poorer it's not really the money they are talking about. It's more about the rich side of life or good days and bad days. Which are necessary for one to be true to themselves.

If you never have a bad day, how will you appreciate the good ones. It's the same with your marriage, there are good days and bad days and just like for yourself these days are necessary in your marriage. Just think about when you were young. You wanted something so bad you would do whatever it takes to get that prize and then when you did you stopped doing what it takes. Same thing in your marriage. You stop thinking about what it takes, and you start to focus on what it takes and now that you have your prize you no longer want to do what it takes.

Well, the good news is, so did she/he. The better news is now no one cares, and every day gets harder and harder until someone breaks the vow.

The children are now the recipients of this wonderful agreement into which they were born. And you wonder why our children are the way they are because we showed them how to act when we are not happy or when we don't want to be somewhere we don't want to be. We flee. We get up and go and half the time we don't even care where we go, we just go.

Misconceptions can play a super big part in our mindset of what is really going on with our significant other. You never really know if they are feeling bad if someone made them angry or they just want some alone time. Either way we assume to have all the answers. We don't and we never will. What we do have is a shoulder, a hug, a mouth that can be used to console one another. We have a way to make them feel better, but never should we assume we have all the answers. What if the answer was no answer? What if we just need to listen and don't speak. How simple is that.

Finding time to do what is needed for someone else can be difficult and can only be effective if you yourself are in a good place. Not when you are stressed from the day or even tired, when you are ready by ready otherwise don't bother it will be perceived as fake news.

One day at a time is the best you can do. Tell your spouse that the next time they need time alone to just say, they need time alone. Plain English really does work.

The end of a new marriage can be made clear when everyone around you decides your marriage is not what it's supposed to be, and they start to tell you what is wrong in your marriage. They have no idea what they are talking about so why does everyone compare to what someone else says your marriage is supposed to be. I am not the only one who has issues in their marriage. Just because someone is quiet in a marriage and does not make a fuss or leave everything when they get angry does not mean they are happily married. Far from it. It just means they may or may not say it in public and the other person won't get mad.

I want each person you know who is married to tell you what they like and don't like in their marriage then you can compare. The truth is somewhere in between.

If there is a need for someone to leave the home for a day or two, let it be the man of the house. Why because that is what men do. They leave the house to the woman. If the woman is the man of the house, then they should leave. Right? or not right? How does this play out in the end? It's just like it started. One is not the man or the woman, each has their place in the relationship and together they play house. One fills in when the other can't and vice versa. How simple is that? Just do what is needed and don't keep score because if you do, nobody will win.

Chapter Four

Follow The Leader

The one who speaks the loudest is normally declared the winner or leader shall I say, but what does that really mean? The one who has all the answers and never waits for a response is the one who thinks they have made an adult decision on behalf of the couple or family. Not only does that make the other party crazy, but it also creates a non-participating person. Who wants to be in a conversation that is not a two way conversation or thoughts are not considered or in some cases cared about.

The real leader is the one who sits back and does nothing. They are the party that has the best interest in mind. There is no real answer in the anger portion of a discrepancy, the answer lies in the discussion and understanding of the real underlying problem, whatever that might be. The more you listen the more you learn the more you can work on helping each other.

One more person that can lead you is God, but unless you have a relationship with God, how will you learn to hear the guidance that is available to you. A marriage can be a great one, but you must know the great one to be married to the right person at the right time and for the right reasons. How will you work through what we on our own cannot?

You can have too much God in a Marriage, but you can't have a marriage without God. Physically you can but the spiritual side of us will be in constant battle with the temptations of life and can only be tamed by the grace of God.

There can never be too much grace in a marriage.

Chapter Five

Bible References to Marriage

When the day starts and you are not sure if you want to stay in the marriage you are in, the first thing you can do is ask God.

You can read the Bible and then pray for help, guidance and even divorce if you are in any kind of abusive situation. There is nowhere in the Bible where it tells you to get beat up or sit there and be yelled at and called names. There just isn't.

The real purpose of God in your marriage is not so that you can be the head of the household but so you can lead the household according to his will.

The first-place winner does not get a blue ribbon, they get a way to live a peaceful life with someone they care about deeply.

Trials will come but they do not have to be the end of the marriage if you don't want it to be but if you do, then it will. Your emotions and actions will display that even when you think they are not. An intuitive feeling will come and tell you it's over. Come to God when things get tough and see how he will smooth things over with you and your spouse. There are many times when you want too much God in your marriage and times when you just need a little. Never let God be the reason for displays of emotions that are negative. Let God be the reason for adult conversations that lead to better days and better nights not separation of duties.

Here are a few key Bible verses for a better marriage:

Hebrews 13:4 - Let **marriage** be held in honor among all, and let the marriage bed be undefiled, for God will judge the sexually immoral and adulterous.

Proverbs 18:22 - He who finds a wife finds a good thing and obtains favor from the Lord.

Genesis 2:24 - Therefore a man shall leave his father and his mother and hold fast to his wife, and they shall become one flesh.

1 Corinthians 13:4-7 - **Love is patient** and kind; love does not envy or boast; it is not arrogant or rude. It does not insist on its own way; it is not irritable or resentful; it does not rejoice at wrongdoing but rejoices with the truth. Love bears all things, believes all things, hopes all things, endures all things.

Of course, these are all written by men of the past, but these can still be applied to the relationships of today.

Chapter Six

The Blind Leading the Blind

This person you have chosen to be your wedding partner is still your partner even if you can't see it right away. The blind one is the one who thinks they are the ones in control.

One way to open your eyes to the truth is to tell the truth to yourself and to your spouse. Why lie about anything? You may have many versions of the truth but only one of them is the truth so use that one. No matter what, tell the truth. How does anyone work things out for the better if you're living a lie. Tell the truth sooner and get all the benefits of doing so. No version of the truth will make a difference if you can't tell the truth from a lie, which many have started to believe their own lies.

The back side of a lie will always circle back, and you are not in a position to stop it once you go down this path, you just backslide.

Stop asking for money for things that you want that do not work for both of you. Example a set of pots and pans is a good thing to use family money on. But a hat for the club when you can't pay your light bill is not a good idea. Be sensible, not overly spending on things that have no meaning and only set you back.

Start contributing to the money pot when you can. There is no reason both partners should not be helping financially. Who said, "What's mine is mine and what's yours is mine?" They lied. Not only did they lie, but they also died broke.

Many people who are in marriages are not happy, but they are doing nothing to make it better and if there is no effort, there is no change and change is exactly what is needed. Here are a few options before calling it quits:

Take a walk together and talk.

Make your favorite meal with a glass of wine or beverage of your choice.

Ask if there is anything you can do to help the situation.

Try not to place blame and focus on improvements, do not blame each other for why you are where you are.

Ask to sit alone from time to time without interruptions.

Be nice to each other.

Help with chores and bills.

Take a break from work and work on you.

Temperments can make things worse, be even tempered and talk things over a little at a time. Try not to solve everything in one day.

Tell each other what you want from them and what you don't want. Mind readers you are not.

Chapter Seven

The Pillars of God and Marriage

After all is said and done, the best way to move forward is to align with God independently but not completely, meaning leave room for the one you love. He/She will always be a part of you even if you are not living together. I AM will make sure you end up with the person that was meant for you and when he does, there is nothing that can keep you apart.

The part that God plays in your marriage can look like someone is driving you apart but really he is asking you to move on. Not every relationship was meant for marriage. Some were to learn things about yourself and to teach someone else in various things.

The first pillar is don't get married if you already have expectations of the other person. The only one who will get what is expected is God. It may look like a competition but it's not. Not even close.

When one person has expectations of the other the only outcome is disappointment.

The second pillar is, keep your hands to yourself. Once you decide to have an affair or even think of having one, you are already creating the wrong outcome of the relationship. There is no right or wrong way to handle your marital issues but adding another party to the mix does not make a good cocktail.

The third pillar will make you want to scream, just scream but not at each other.

Ask for help but please don't demand anything or you will get less than the first ask.

Seek counseling from God through Christ and then together listen for the answers.

Sit by yourself for your own directions as each person has their own reason for love to have created them.

Make choices that benefit each other and yourself not the other way around.

Alignment is all about proper order. God first, then you as God's child, Spouse and Children are next.

Make the best of what you have and ask God for what you don't.

Send your love through your words, actions, and body language not your middle finger, your wicked tongue and separation.

Make God your priority and he will make you his.

Chapter Eight

When All Is Said and Done

When all is said and done and you're still wondering what happened, just know it happened for a reason. What did you learn? What did you make and why? Who will fill those shoes now? Make sure you get answers to those kinds of questions, so you don't have to do it all again.

The end of one situation is not the real end, it's a transition event to your next life lesson.

God is not competing with you; God is your creator and knows the desires of your heart. There lies the real challenge.

Evaluating the heart and the mind will follow for the other direction will create the opposite and the battle will only get harder.

If you are in a marriage you don't want to be in, you won't be even if you keep saying you are. Take your time and be where you want to be for the benefit of you both. The children will figure it out sooner than later.

About The Author

He has served as a Project Manager for one of the City of Philadelphia's Public Housing HOPE VI redevelopment projects valued at $52 million. Mr. Johnakin's involvement forced the local Housing Authority, property developers, and general contractors to actively engage in the training and hiring of residents, in accordance with Section 3 of the Housing and Urban Development Act of 1968, as amended. He has attracted the ears of those in local government by bringing a source of reason and advocacy to the cause of economic development in distressed communities; this includes testifying before the Philadelphia City Council on multiple occasions. He has served as an economic development consultant for Universal Community Homes, a multi-million-dollar community development enterprise started by world-renowned music composer and legend, Mr. Kenny Gamble.

His professional affiliations include but are not limited to: Omega Psi Phi Fraternity, Inc., Mason Hiram #5 and Shriner Pyramid #1. Additionally, he has been presented with numerous community service awards including the Men Making a Difference Award, presented by the former U.S. Representative Chaka Fattah (D-PA).

Mr. Johnakin received a Bachelor of Science in Recreation Leisure Management (Magna Cum Laude) – minor in Sociology from Cheyney University, Cheyney, PA; a Master's Degree Business Systems (MBS) - Concentration Human Resources & Entrepreneurship, from Lincoln University, Coatesville, PA; and is a Doctoral Candidate in Business - Concentration Urban Planning, from Walden University, Baltimore, MD.

www.ingramcontent.com/pod-product-compliance
Lightning Source LLC
Chambersburg PA
CBHW022007100426
42738CB00041B/952

"Inviting us to question what we may have been told in religious traditions, Joanne Swenson encourages us to discover our own deepest questions about spiritual power and meaning. This is the liberating invitation that young minds need."

—ELAINE PAGELS,
Harrington Spear Paine Professor of Religion,
Princeton University

"That a Harvard-trained scholar writes so accessibly—in lessons to her adult children—is refreshing. *Eight Trails* is a wise, thoughtful companion for anyone seeking meaning and purpose. Swenson's brilliant trail metaphor turns key attributes into lived experience, offering clarity and spiritual depth. Even at my age of seventy-seven, reading it sparked deep introspection. It felt like walking familiar ground and suddenly noticing important markers I'd missed. This book guides readers of all ages toward a life anchored in meaningful religious commitments."

—FRED SIEVERT,
Retired President, New York Life Insurance Company

"Joanne Swenson's *Eight Trails* will be a valuable tool for anyone talking to an often-skeptical younger generation about the nature of religious faith. Drawing upon her family's history of trips in the Pacific Northwest and her experiences from teaching world religions, it is an engaging and refreshing look at faith without relying on too-familiar tropes."

—JOHN W. HAWTHORNE,
author of *The Fearless Christian University*

"*Eight Trails* is a wise and timely guide for anyone who feels lost on their spiritual path. With depth, humility, and grace, Rev. Joanne Swenson shows how religious faith—when approached with curiosity and courage—can still illuminate the way. A profound companion for seekers and skeptics alike."

—BRANDAN ROBERTSON,
author of *Queer and Christian: Reclaiming the Bible, Our Faith, and Our Place at the Table*